This book belongs to:

_____

WILD ONES

Emperor
PENGUINS

by JILL ANDERSON

NorthWord
Minnetonka, Minnesota

It is winter in Antarctica.

Hundreds of black-and-white birds huddle together in the icy wind.

These are
daddy emperor penguins,
and each of them
is hiding a

sec et.

Under a furry flap
of belly skin,
there's a...

Emperors are
the largest kind
of penguin.
There are 17 kinds
in all, but only
emperors and
Adélie penguins live
in Antarctica.

Raising a chick in such a cold place takes careful planning.

First, each mother penguin lays one egg. She quickly rolls the egg onto the father's warm feet. Then the females start off on a long journey to the sea.

Once the females reach the water, they use their wings like flippers to swim fast and dive deep.

Their long, thin beak and prickly tongue are great for catching fish and squid.

When their tummies are full, the females make the long trip back. Two months have passed, and their **chicks** have **hatched!**

Now it's the mommies' turn to watch their young. They spit up some food for their babies to eat. Then the males head to the ocean to find food. They are **very** hungry.

The water of the Antarctic is **very cold**, but penguins don't mind. They have a thick layer of fat to hold in heat, and oily feathers that keep water away from their skin.

In the spring all the chicks run and play together.

Parents are the only ones who feed their chick, but all the adults take turns babysitting.

By summertime, the young penguins' fluffy feathers are sleek and waterproof.

They head for the water, and **WHOOSH!** Off they swim in search of a fishy feast.

For Dad, who would
weather any storm for me
—J. A.

Composed in the United States of America
Designed by Lois A. Rainwater • Edited by Kristen McCurry

Text © 2007 by Jill Anderson

NORTHWORD
Books for Young Readers
11571 K-Tel Drive
Minnetonka, MN 55343
www.tnkidsbooks.com

Photographs © 2007 provided by:
Frans Lanting/Minden Pictures: cover, endsheets, pp. 5, 9, 10-11, 17, 20-21;
Guillaume Dargaud: pp. 1, 2-3, 6, 7, 8, 14, 15; Shutterstock: back cover, p. 4; Ingo Arndt/Minden Pictures: pp. 12-13;
Norbert Wu/Minden Pictures: pp. 13 (fish), 22-23; Hiroya Minakuchi/Minden Pictures: p. 16;
Graham Robertson/Auscape/Minden Pictures: pp. 18-19; Konrad Wothe/Minden Pictures: p. 24.

Library of Congress Cataloging-in-Publication Data

Anderson, Jill.
Emperor penguins / by Jill Anderson.
p. cm. -- (Wild ones)
ISBN 978-1-55971-972-8 (hc) -- ISBN 978-1-55971-973-5 (sc)
1. Emperor penguin--Juvenile literature. I. Title.

QL696.S473A47 2007

598.4'4--dc22   2006101494

Printed in Singapore
10 9 8 7 6 5 4 3 2 1